I CAN

DISCOVER YOUR POWER WITHIN

RYUHO OKAWA

HS PRESS

Copyright © 2019 by Ryuho Okawa
Original title: "I Can! Watashiwa Dekiru!"
HS Press is an imprint of IRH Press Co., Ltd.
Tokyo
ISBN 13: 978-1-943928-38-5
ISBN 10: 1-943928-38-X
Printed in the United States of America
First Edition (updated)

Contents

Preface 9

1
You Have the
Power of God Within

1 What it Means to be a Child of God 12

2 The Kingdom of God Within You 16

3 The Possibility in Thinking 22

4 Dream On Behalf of God 25

2
The Importance of Self-Help Thinking

1 God Helps Those Who Help Themselves 30

2 The Power from Heaven and the Power from Within .. 35

3 Separate Self-Help Thinking from Fatalism 38

4 Environmentalism is Nothing But an Excuse 40

5 Accumulation Leads to "the Shift" 44

6 Bring Out the Diamond in You 47

3
How to Become a Creative Person

1 You Need a Hidden Period for Production 50

2 The Power of Accumulation 54

3 Inspiration Comes As a Result of Your Efforts 58

4 Having Sacred Desire is the Starting Point 62

5 Focus On Your Strong Point 64

4
I Can
– The Key to Life's Golden Secrets

1 "I Can" is a Magical Phrase 68

2 The Key is to Take Control of Your Mind 70

3 What You Think is What You Are 74

4 Make Up Your Mind and Design a Beautiful Future ... 78

Afterword 83

* The lectures were conducted in English.

About the Author 85

What is El Cantare? 86

About Happy Science 88

Contact Information 92

About HS Press 94

Books by Ryuho Okawa 95

Music by Ryuho Okawa 100

Preface

This book will lead your future to success.

In a very simple way, I revealed the secret to how I, myself, became successful.

By reading this single book deeply, your success rate will increase by more than tenfold.

Of course, this teaching is just a part of God's teachings. But it is an exciting experience that you, yourself, can become a "small creator" through your faith in God.

I, myself, started from a small belief in myself, and became a world visionary with many believers in more than 100 countries all over the world. In this book, you can discover the basic theory for that.

Ryuho Okawa
Master & CEO of Happy Science Group
Aug. 22, 2019

1

You Have the Power of God Within

June 15, 2012 at Happy Science General Headquarters, Tokyo

1

What it Means to be A Child of God

The Christian and Buddhist interpretations

Today's subject is, "You Have the Power of God Within." It's a little different sound you feel from this subject, the theme. Why? You are just humankind, men or women. Why do you have the power of God within? Is it speaking too much? Are you highly appreciated? Is it too much? Too much words? Will it invite punishment from the heavenly world? Are you going to be persecuted from Christian churches because I said, "You have the power of God within"? "You have the power of God within" means you look just like Jesus Christ.

Historically, in Christianity, usually, "Son of God" means Jesus Christ only. However, the Japanese people easily accept the thinking that "You are the children of God," because they were taught in their history that they are children of Buddha. When they learned Buddhism that came from India through China, Korea, or south part of Asia, they learned like that.

Buddha historically taught that firstly, Buddha himself didn't start from Buddha, I mean the Awakened One, Savior, or God Himself. He recognized himself as one of the pursuers of the Truth. At the time, there were a lot of people who were seeking for the Truth of God or the Truth of Buddha. In India, more than 2,500 years ago, when a person made great efforts to attain enlightenment, that person got awakened and had something in him or her to know the secret of the world and the secret of himself or herself. At that time, when the person became an Awakened One, that meant he or she became a buddha. It means he was just awakened. To be awakened means to become a buddha.

Someone with God-like nature within him

In other words, in the occidental context, it means to become the "Son of God" or something like that. The meaning of the Son of God, in this context, is someone who has almost the same nature of God within him. So, the oriental way of thinking and awakening are a little different from the occidental way of thinking and method of disciplining themselves.

But from a different standpoint of thinking, in Buddhism, there is also the attitude of democracy-like religion. So, Japanese people easily understand the words, "to be a child of God," but in the western history, people who devoted themselves to God or churches did not easily accept phrases like, "...who have the power of God within." They sometimes think that these are words of Satan or someone like that, these will lead you to the wrong way, or it will mislead you to hell. They usually think like that.

2

The Kingdom of God Within You

Finding Truth, goodness, and beauty in you

But I really want to say to you that, "You have the power of God within" means that "You have the Kingdom of God within you." It is easier to understand than the words, "You have the power of God within." "You have the Kingdom of God within you" is a little easier for all of you. What does "the Kingdom of God" mean? "Kingdom" means the area or realm of God. Think deeply inside of you, and at that time, you will find something beautiful in your mind, something good in you, or finally something eternal.

Then, today, I want to talk to you about this kind of kingdom, area, or realm of God within you. What is "the Kingdom of God in you"?

In religion, faith is the bridge from men to God. When you have ardent and deep faith in God, your mind will combine to the heart of God in heaven. It means you have goodness, beauty, or Truth in you. I want to say to you, while you are keeping a peaceful mind in you with good faith, you are near God, or in some meaning, you can be a neighbor to God.

But you are sometimes easily disappointed with yourself because you, as a human, are apt to make a lot of mistakes and you've experienced a lot of disappointment in your own history. So, you'll feel hesitant to accept this kind of thinking.

Of course, human beings have a tendency to make a mistake. There is an old saying, "To err is human, to forgive divine," which means that human beings usually make a lot of mistakes, but only God has the right to forgive them all. It's the traditional meaning of faith and the traditional acceptance of religion.

The creator in you

But now, from the end of the 19th century, through the 20th century, to the 21st century, man has a different kind of power. It was found by some kind of bright-side* liking people, the people who aimed at making a successful life by their own power, for themselves. Such kind of people were produced during the 20th century, and now, this is still going on especially in the United States of America. Such influence came to Europe, Japan, and some Americanized coun-tries in the world.

So, here is one starting point you should stand when you are thinking about the Kingdom of God within you. This theory, in other words, says that

---

* A religious and philosophical movement called the New Thought movement occurred in the U.S. in the 19th century. Many of the groups are Christian, and they basically hold the positive thinking that "good thoughts lead to good things." Napoleon Hill's philosophy of success, Norman Vincent Peale's positive thinking, and Joseph Murphy's rules for success using the subconscious, which are ideas in the 20th century, are just a few examples of this movement.

you are what you are thinking about, and what you are thinking about all day long. Famous President Lincoln already knew about that. Of course, these are the famous words of Napoleon Hill, the philosopher of a successful mind in growing rich. In the old times, the same thing was taught by Buddha, Socrates, Marcus Aurelius, and others like them. That is the essence of the mind.

You have a creator in you. This "creator," of course, doesn't mean you made the Sun, the Moon, the Earth, or the stars, that is too much. You can create these things in the planetarium, of course, but in reality, it's a little difficult, I guess. But you can imagine a lot of things in you, and what you imagine in you itself is the possibility of designing, building, and realizing, your plan or your dream.

Your dream is your life plan

"Dreams come true" is a truth. If you have the ability to dream in you, it means you have the possibility to realize your dream. A dream is just the plan for your life. If you can dream, you can make plans in your life, and these plans will lead you to the future and make your future.

Your dream will make it easier for you to do your daily efforts. Because you have the final goal in you, you can clearly look at your final goal, so what is required of your efforts is limited. They are great efforts, I guess, but such great efforts, in your mind, must be limited because you already found your final goal thanks to your ability to dream.

If you can set your final goal, you can calculate how long or how intensely you should make efforts. So, you must divide those efforts day by day, and you should do your best in one day, the twenty-four hours. If you do, your dream will surely come true, in the near future or before you pass away from this world.

3

The Possibility in Thinking

Imagine your final goal

Then, the point is the possibility in thinking. The possibility in thinking is the starting point to find the Kingdom of God within you. If you can think about the Kingdom of God in you, it means you can find your own destiny or your own final goal.

If you can imagine such kind of final goal, and shall this final goal be accepted by God, in other words, if God blesses your dream or your final goal, it means it is possible, indeed possible. If God welcomes you or your dreams, it will be possible to think like that. Your dream shall come true.

You are creating the world
As a substitute for God

You have a possibility in you, the possibility in your thinking, the possibility of what you think about all day long. That is what makes the difference between one person and another. It will distinguish a person with a religious personality from other common people.

If you can think about God in your mind every day, or all day long, it means you are sitting near God, and you are a substitute for God in creating this world. If it's a small part of the world or not, is not so great a thing. A small thing is a big thing, and a big thing is a small thing. Small people shall be greater people, and greater people shall be smaller people in the world of God.

So, just look inside your brain, heart, or mind, guess what you can be, and imagine that you are so. That possibility will mean that you can be a part of God. This is another meaning of the "Son of God."

So, it might be a little different from the historical Christianity or the concept of thinking of the Roman Catholic or another form of Christianity, but I think that Buddhism's "child of Buddha" is almost equal to the "child of God" in Christianity. "You have the power of God within" means "You have the power of Buddha within." It is a possibility.

4

Dream On Behalf of God

*Your power of imagination
Is the possibility of your soul*

You have already received everything in you. You can, of course, imagine your miserable situation, inferiority complex, or disappointing self-history. It is easy to say so. But at the same time, you have a golden life with you. You have been given everything from God. You already received your own life, and this "life" means your soul.

You have a soul. It is the prerequisite for the idea, "You are a child of God." If you have a soul, it comes from God's will, and this means you have a responsibility in this world to make the world a utopia instead of God doing the work himself.

So, you have a possibility, an imagining power. This imagining power means you have a possibility, and your possibility will lead you to the seat next to God.

Jesus Christ is a great person in history, and is almost God, of course, but he, himself, was historically a human. This kind of human awakened and received revelations from God, and awakened to the fact that he was a savior. At that time, he became the "Son of God," I think. Every religion thinks that it is the best one in the world, so Jesus Christ must be the best one in the history of humans in Christianity. It's OK for Christian people, that Jesus Christ is the only one who was given the power of God. It's possible to think like that. But there are a lot of religions in the world, and there are a lot of saviors in the world, historically.

With the power of God, Everything is possible

So, I think the starting point is, what you are thinking in your mind. Look at that, and if you can think like how God thinks, it means you are a child of God and you have the power of God within.

This power of God leads you everywhere. Because you have love in you, you can love other people. It's one of the powers of God. You can have mercy on the miserable people, people who suffer from illness, or people who are in great difficulties in inner-country conflicts nowadays. You can have compassion for them. It's also one of the powers of God, I think. You can give hope to them, you can assist and aid them to rebuild their own countries. You can share your dream with other people of foreign countries. It must be one of the powers of God, too.

Of course, when you study a lot in your life, you will naturally seek to get the real Truth. This tendency is included in your life.

You have a tendency to get the Truth.
You have a desire to get the Truth.
You have an aspiration to get the Truth.
You have a dream
To have better and better dreams.
All these thinking attitudes belong to God.
So, you have the kingdom within you,
And you have the power of God within.
This means the possibility in dreaming.
Dream of God.
Dream on behalf of God.
Dream when you awaken to
Your own destiny.
That is the conclusion.

2

The Importance of Self-Help Thinking

May 31, 2012 at Happy Science General Headquarters, Tokyo

1

God Helps Those Who Help Themselves

The Secret behind The Industrial Revolution in the U.K.

Today, I want to speak about "The Importance of Self-Help Thinking." It was requested from our International Division (currently International Headquarters) because a lot of people who are living in Africa and Asia are apt to think that faith is a given benefit from God, and that if you have some kind of faith, you can receive or expect some kind of benefit from God. "This is the style of religion," they are apt to think like that. But we, Happy Science, teach a lot of different contents in our teachings.

The Importance of Self-Help Thinking

First of all, I will teach you about the meaning of self-help thinking. There is a famous saying, "God helps those who help themselves." It's very famous. Today's lecture is regarding this saying, as you know.

Almost 140 years ago, in the early period of the Meiji Restoration, there was one book which was brought from the United Kingdom and translated into Japanese. The famous book's name was *Self-Help*, written by Samuel Smiles[*], a British.

We, the Japanese people, have high evaluation for the Meiji Restoration. Before the Meiji Restoration, there was the Edo Bakufu regime, and in its last period, one of the most excellent students went abroad to the United Kingdom to study

---

[*] Samuel Smiles (1812 ~ 1904) was a Scottish author and doctor, known for his writings such as *Self-Help* (published in 1859) and *Character* (published in 1871).

the secret of the Industrial Revolution in the U.K. and why it became the number one country at that time. His name was Masanao Nakamura*, sometimes called Seichoku Nakamura. Mr. Nakamura studied hard, but he couldn't find the reason for the success of the U.K., the sudden and rapid growth and emergence of the United Kingdom in respect to its industry.

During his studying period occurred the Meiji Restoration, a famous, non-blood revolution that occurred in Japan. He was sent to the U.K. by the Edo Bakufu authority, so he had to come back to Japan, and when he said farewell to his friend in the U.K., he was given one book; it was *Self-Help*. It sold 100,000 copies in the U.K. at that time. It was a bestseller, but Mr. Nakamura didn't know about

---

* Masanao Nakamura (1832 ~ 1891) was a Japanese enlightener and educator in the Meiji period. With Nakamura as the supervisor, he and Japanese students were sent to England by the Edo shogunate, from 1866 to 1868. In 1870, he published the Japanese translated version of *Self-Help* titled, *Saigoku Risshi Hen*. He later became a professor of Faculty of Letters at the University of Tokyo.

that book. He read this book, again and again in the ship, almost to the point where he could remember all the pages in it.

Almost all intelligent people of Japan Had read Self-Help

When he came back to Japan, there had been proceeding a lot of revolutionary phenomena. So, he translated the book, *Self-Help* into Japanese at a rapid speed. This was very important. At that time, he translated "self-help" into Japanese to mean "aspiration," not "self-help," but "aspiration." He translated its theme as "The Aspiration of Western People."

At that time, the reading population, or people who can read books, was estimated at one million or so, and *Self-Help* was read more than one million copies, so it's said that almost all Japanese intelligent people studied this book. It was one of the main engines of the Meiji period, and Japan made a lot of progress through this book.

2

The Power from Heaven and The Power from Within

A miracle occurs
When the two powers combine

So, I dare say that you need religion, of course, and it requires belief, of course. Belief includes some kind of good news from God, or a miraculous phenomenon.

But in the beginning, I already said that God saves those who want to save themselves. It's true. There can be two kinds of directions of power. One is the power from heaven, which is a mercy of God, and the other one is the power which comes from within a human being, himself. These two powers combine into one power, and at that time, there appears a miracle in your life.

This world is a school

So, don't only wait for the good news or good phenomenon from God or the heavenly world. You should do for yourself, as far as you can do. God also blesses you, who are aiming at succeeding in your lives by dint of your own ability or efforts. It will win the appreciation of God because you, human beings, come to this world as trainees who forget the real memory of heaven and who you were.

So, this life is the training period, this world is just a school of human life. In every school, teachers have to teach a lot of things regarding the Truth, but students also must study harder and harder on their side. These two efforts are very welcomed.

So, I want to say to the people who are apt to say that, "We are unhappy," "I am unhappy," or "Unfortunately I cannot succeed in my life," to stop speaking like that.

Just think about your efforts first, and there will follow the assistance or aid of gods after that. This is the importance of self-help.

3

Separate Self-Help Thinking From Fatalism

Do good things,
But refrain from doing bad things

Secondly, self-help thinking must be separated from fatalism. Fatalism is one of the beliefs that say your fate in this world had been determined already when you were born in this world. This is fatalism.

People say that it's difficult to change your fate because it's already determined, but I usually say that we have the laws of cause and effect. The laws of cause and effect mean that if you do good things, you can receive good things, and if you do bad things, you will be punished in some way. So, do good things and hesitate to do bad things, and there will appear your real consciousness. Your real consciousness will lead your life to a better one.

So, please keep distance between self-help thinking and fatalism. The attitude is very important. If there is fatalism or not, or if it is true or not, don't think too much about that; just think about self-help thinking.

4
Environmentalism Is Nothing But an Excuse

You already knew about your environment Before you were born

Thirdly, next to fatalism comes environmen-talism. It is a theory that says human beings should be conditioned by the environment because they cannot choose their birthplace, meaning the country, or their parents, brothers and sisters, friends, or the occupation of their parents.

This kind of thinking is usual nowadays, but I already taught that, before you came from heaven, you already knew about your environment and your birthplace—your human condition—when you were born. So, it's just an excuse, it leads you nowhere. It's not a successful attitude. You can explain about your bad environment, breeding atmosphere, or as a result, your educational background, or your money background, things like that. But these are just complaints.

You can choose a lot of ways, and you need to make decisions at that time. If you have an aspiration—in this context, it means self-help thinking—to do something, you can open your way to success.

You can gain knowledge
Even if you have no educational background

For example, one point is your educational background. It is sometimes used as an explanation of your being unpromoted, as the reason you cannot enter a great company, for your having a low salary, or things like that.

But please look back on history and remember, for example, President Lincoln or Thomas Edison, and in Japan, Konosuke Matsushita.

Mr. Matsushita could not finish elementary school, but he made a worldwide company, now the well-known Panasonic. So, even if you don't have enough educational background, it's just an excuse.

If you want knowledge, you can get it. Wisdom is very welcomed these days, but wisdom comes from a lot of knowledge; knowledge can be learned by studying; and studying means reading a lot of books or getting a lot of information. So, it depends on your effort. Make effort to get knowledge. It's important.

Ideas come from knowledge, Experience and adversity

The next energy of the future society is not oil, gas, plutonium, or things like that. The next energy must be ideas. Ideas will make new industries, so you must seek to get ideas.

Ideas come from knowledge, or accompanied by knowledge, and grow through experience.

What kind of experience do you imagine? This "experience" is a sort of adversity, meaning a bad condition or unusual difficulty. If you can get through an unusual condition or a bad condition through your knowledge, "knowledge is power" and it will turn into wisdom at that time.

Ideas come from knowledge, and knowledge comes from reading and experience. These are available through your daily efforts. It's very important.

Do nothing and you will get nothing. Do anything and you can expect something you want to get. Your effort will not be fruitful in a short period, but in the long run, it will bear fruits. So, make efforts every day, day by day. It's very important.

5

Accumulation Leads to "The Shift"

Life is a succession of "todays"

The most important thing is that life is successive days of one day, or "today." Yesterday was "today" of the day before, today is "today," and tomorrow is "today" of the next day. Therefore, life is like the chain of "todays," that is what I mean.

So, the next word I must say is "accumulation." The importance of accumulation, I cannot emphasize enough. If you get one knowledge, it might not produce a lot of fruits, but if you get knowledge day by day and accumulate it, there should come the tipping point.

The Importance of Self-Help Thinking

You need only effort, day by day

"The shift" will occur at that point, on that day. Someday, it will make the shift occur. The shift is the change in your life, change in your mind, and change in your attitude. At that time, you can turn to a different direction and will become a different person.

The shift will occur. It's a "quantum moment," the words of Dr. Wayne Dyer. Quantum moment comes from "quantum leap" in physics. Sometimes, your accumulation of knowledge will turn into quite a different one, and at that time, bear beautiful fruits. No one knows the time, or when it will occur, but someday, there must be that kind of a shift. The shift time will come, and you can be a different person at that time.

You need only effort, day by day, and your effort will produce you a lot of ideas. Ideas are the next energy of the next, coming age. Ideas will be the new, added value to your work—you must get ideas by getting different viewpoints in your life.

6

Bring Out the Diamond In You

Believe in self-help thinking

So, self-help thinking means "how to educate yourself." The English word "educate" originally comes from Latin that means "to pull out something valuable that is inside of you." Education is the act of pulling out your diamond that is inside of you. So, self-help thinking will make you greater and greater, and you can become quite a different person.

I, myself, have accumulated a lot of knowledge through these 55 years, and this accumulation of knowledge made me quite different from other people. I have a lot of resources for ideas. I'm one of the most resourceful people in Japan and in the world. It comes from my daily efforts.

Your daily efforts and your accumulation of knowledge will change your life in the near future. The shift will occur at that time, and you can be quite a different person. You can lead a successful life at that time.

So, please believe in self-help thinking.
You should part from fatalism.
You should part from environmentalism.
You should stop explaining about something,
Stop speaking ill of others,
And stop seeking for reasons of your unhappiness.
You can make yourself better and better
By dint of your own efforts.
I promise this Truth.

3

How to Become a Creative Person

August 26, 2011 at Happy Science General Headquarters, Tokyo

1

You Need a Hidden Period For Production

Cicadas live in the earth for several years
Just to live on the surface for seven days

It is late summer in Japan. There sounds a lot of music of cicada around here. I had one idea this morning that these cicadas, or semi in Japanese, have been living in the earth for several years and after that, they appeared to the surface of the soil, the earth. That is when, for the first time, they met the scenery of the surroundings and the environment of the earth, and saw sunshine.

However, it is said that they can live for only seven days in this earthly world. There was a movie this year (2011), its name was literally *A Cicada of the Eighth Day*, or for the Japanese people, *Youka-*

me-no-Semi. Since a cicada lives for only seven days, on the eighth day, it is almost a dead body or must be dead. It means the last day of the character's life.

The inspiration from the story was that, when we can make or produce something profitable, meaning something which adds some value we have not created till now, we need a hidden period for the preparation of production. Even cicadas need several years before they can fly around the earth and in the air, sing a lot of music, and produce the atmosphere of the late summer for one week. We, human beings, cannot understand their music, but they will tell you that, "Your last day is coming. What is your question or your problem? You must solve the problem before the end of the day." They want to tell you about that. If you want to tell the answers of your workbook of life, you need a lot of years to prepare to make a music of your life and sing it to other people for them to hear.

It took me 30 years to be able to give All kinds of teachings

So firstly, I dare say that today's theme is "How to Become a Creative Person," and the first point of this theme is that you need a hidden period for preparation to create something important for human beings.

For example, if you are working for a religious group, and if you want to become good and well-known religious people who can make great influence on other people, you need a lot of preparation for that. You need many years of studying, of course. Like the cicadas, you need several years for only seven days of music.

As for me, I studied about the spiritual world for more than 30 years, and now I can tell you from a lot of angles about the spiritual world and the teachings. It took 30 years, even for me, to teach a lot of things from a lot of standpoints. So firstly, you need hidden periods for preparation to become a great person, which includes becoming a creative person.

2

The Power of Accumulation

Study Buddha's Truth
And collect information

What is a creative person? It is a person who assists or makes some efforts to create a brave new world. If you are old-fashioned people, you cannot make anything, and you can add almost nothing to this world. In the world from now on, you can produce any products regarding Buddha's Truth. So firstly, you are required, in other words, waiting time, and during that time, you are required to make a lot of effort.

This effort, of course, means to study Buddha's Truth. In addition to that, I dare say that you must know a lot of new intelligence about this world. It's the beginning of a new world, and of course, ancient history of the world regarding Japan and other countries. If you are oriented to start dendo (missionary work) to foreign countries, you must know about their histories, of course, and about their thoughts and opinions.

A small piece of hour
Will make you greater

So, the second point I want to say is that you are required to know a lot of things. It is easier said than done. It is easy to say to study harder and harder, but not so easy to do.

It's everyday work. You must believe in the accumulative power, the accumulative effects of studying. Every day, each day, you study, for example, 10 minutes or 15 minutes. This is a slow walk and you can make a little result from that, but another day, another year, two years, or three years shall pass like an arrow, so at that time, you will have become quite a different person, and you will have a lot of knowledge regarding what you are oriented to.

So, please believe in the cumulative effect or cumulative power. Don't disregard or think little of that. It's very important. I, myself, made such kind of small efforts every day in these 30 years, and it led me to teach you a lot of stories, including English speeches.

So, I must tell you that the small piece of hour is very essential for you to improve yourself and to make you greater and greater. If you disregard such small part of time, "This is just 10 minutes," "This is just 15 minutes," or "I can do nothing, it's a disposable time, so I cannot think much of that time. I can have fun at that time," it's easy for you, but it leads you to the common person, usual person who lives anywhere around the world.

These small accumulations will lead you to become a greater leader, so don't forget about that. You must know this cumulative effect of your time and efforts. It is very important.

3

Inspiration Comes As a Result of Your Efforts

You need 99 percent perspiration

Thirdly, adding to that, I will tell you that if you are thinking about creation, creative power, or the secret of creation, you might often think that creation must be "inspirationable." You are firstly apt to think that you need some inspiration from heaven. It's true, of course. It's true. If your thought or ideas contain a lot of inspiration from heaven, they might be very creative in every sort of the word.

But it's not so easy to get inspiration from another world. As Edison said, you need 99 percent of perspiration when you want to get

1 percent of inspiration, meaning that 99 percent of perspiration will lead you to or let you get 1 percent of inspiration.

Do you understand what I mean? If you want 1 percent inspiration from the heavenly world, you must do good things by yourself or seek for 1 percent heavenly inspiration as the result of 99 percent perspiration. Perspiration, of course, means effort.

It's true through my experience. It's very true. I'm a very inspirationable person, of course. For example, my speech needs no preparation. I can speak in any case, on every theme, about something regarding Buddha's Truth, but there exists a lot of indirect, or not so direct, effort every day. This is the real meaning of inspiration. Inspiration comes from heaven, only for such a person who is working every day with a lot of perspiration. So, don't forget about that.

Make time for meditation-like rest

If you are fond of practicing meditation, it's a good thing. We are a religious group, so we recommend meditation, of course. If you continue to do meditation, there will occur or come down to you a good idea from heaven, but before that, you need to make a lot of efforts in daily life and in your daily work at your firm or another place. It's a truth.

Then, this is the next point. You must work harder and harder, but sometimes you need meditation-like rest or retreat. You must know these two points.

First is, you must be a diligent person and work harder and harder every day, of course. But it will not lead you to become a creative person. If you want to transform yourself into a creative person, you need some kind of rest, or some sort of meditation or retreat time. If these people, who are thinking harder and harder, working harder and harder, and studying harder and harder, take some rest and do meditation, they can expect some inspiration from heaven. I guarantee that. You need rest before you devise some inspiration or creative power.

4

Having Sacred Desire is The Starting Point

In addition to that, I will teach you about another thought, "Inspirational people are apt to start from some kind of sacred desire." "Sacred desire" sounds different to the people who are living nowadays. Desire, of course, is your imagination of how you should be in the near future. It's easy to imagine, and such sort of books are sold at a lot of bookstores all over the world. But it's not enough. It's not enough.

Imaginative power, of course, produces some kind of result. That's imaginative power. But beyond that imaginative power, we need a sacred desire. If you don't have a sacred desire, you can attract a lot of things, including good things and bad things. The law of the mind attracts everything in the mental world, so you must be sacred in your mind. It means, don't think about yourself too much. Your imaginative world of the future must include a sacred desire or sacred design of the world.

This is the starting point of a religious person. So, if you want to be a religious person, want to get good inspiration from heaven, and want to be empowered with the creative power of God or high spirits, you must begin your work from a sacred desire. Sacred desire includes some kind of abandonment of your earthly desire. You must focus on real important things.

5

Focus On Your Strong Point

The last thing is focusing. If you want to be creative, you must be a person who can focus on the most important thing. Focusing is the royal road to success. Of course, there might be a very talented person who has a lot of abilities. There might be such kind of people. We must bless them, of course. Don't envy such kind of people, we must bless them.

But almost all of us are not so talented, or instead narrow-talented; we have only one strong point in the end. So, you must find that strong point, focus on it, and throw your every effort into that one strong point of yours. That will lead you to contribute something creative in this world, and you can be a power of this world and Happy Science.

So, please remember these things I said today. Some things might be very difficult for you, but I said a lot of things. One thing is, you need a hidden period, and of course, you must make a lot of efforts. You need some sort of rest, or a retreat or meditation period. Don't forget about "99 percent of perspiration leads you to 1 percent of inspiration." Lastly, focusing on your strong point will make you a very creative person. I said such kinds of things.

4

I Can – The Key to Life's Golden Secrets

January 16, 2009 at Happy Science General Headquarters, Tokyo

1

"I Can" is a Magical Phrase

"I can" can make you
A president or a prime minister

Today, I chose the theme, "I Can - The Key to Life's Golden Secrets." This phrase, "I can," is very familiar to you. Of course, it's a well-known phrase because you've heard a lot of this phrase last year on TV, radio, or some other tools.

This is a phrase, of course, the key to the golden secrets of the President of the United States Barack Obama (at the time of the lecture). This phrase, "I can," he used several times: "Yes, I can," "Yes, you can," "Yes, we can," "Yes, we can change, change, change." This is the secret of his success. That's all. That's everything. He said nothing other than that.

These are magical words, "I can," "You can," and "We can." You can be the president of the United States, and of course, you can be the prime minister of Japan. If you want to be a president or a prime minister, please use "I can," "We can," or "Yes, we can." Try, try, and try, again, again, and again.

Historically, these are magical words. We, religious people, know well about these words. They have a magical power in them, so you must know the secret. They are the key to life's golden secrets and success.

2

The Key is to Take Control of Your Mind

An airbus incident
Can be perceived As a miracle

For example, this morning, when I was watching CNN, I just saw a small airbus fall into the Hudson River in New York. When it took off, a flock of geese struck it. Because of the bird strike, the airbus fell down into the river and was floating on it, but a quick rescue by boat saved the lives of more than 150 people. "Immediate rescue," the reporter said.*

---

* On January 15, 2009, US Airways' Airbus A320 crash-landed in the Hudson River, soon after taking off from LaGuardia Airport in New York City. Its engines shut down as a result of a bird strike. All 155 passengers and crew were miraculously rescued.

While I watched TV, I thought about this phrase, "I can." When some people watched this scene on TV, they might have thought that this kind of thing happening at the beginning of the new year is bad luck and it's not a good year. But other people will think, for example, "Oh, it's good news. I know how cold the Hudson River is in New York in January. It's very cold, almost all of them must or should have died. But the report said that it is believed that almost all of them were saved. It's a miracle." Things are changeable by how you think about them, so be careful. This is the real secret and real key to solve your problems in life.

Shift your mind toward
The positive direction

Firstly, I want to ask you, "Please control your mind over how you feel, how you think, and how you judge your daily events, daily occurrences, or daily happenings." It's very important. The point is the attitude of your mind, not the objective-minded thinking. It's up to your own mind. What kind of orientation you, yourself, have is very important.

Barack Obama became the president of the United States, and he used "I can," "You can," but you, yourselves, can use these words, "I can." In real life, a lot of people are confronted with difficulties, but at that time, how you control your thinking is very important. It's the key to your golden life, I want to say so.

I, myself, suffered from a lot of difficulties in my younger days. Even now, I confront a lot of difficulties, but at that time, I just stop thinking and change my mind to the positive direction. "Is there any other thinking?" "Is there possibility thinking?" I ask myself, and at that time, I can find several answers.

You, yourself, might have some kind of difficulties, sufferings, or setbacks, but nothing can defeat you if you have strong belief in you. When you believe in God or in Buddha, or believe in your Lord El Cantare, no one can defeat you, so at that time, be strong and use this magical phrase, "I can." It has real power.

3

What You Think is What You Are

Humans are not material beings,
But spiritual beings

Even in the business world, you can use these words. People who have made a great success in their business sometimes use these magical words, "I can." This is a real magic. It depends on what you think a human being is. Is a human being a material being or a spiritual being? It depends on this choice.

If the real human being is not a material thing and is a spiritual being, what you think is what you are. It's a very deep Truth. What you are thinking about all day long is yourself. You are thinking a lot of things every day, but what you are thinking all day long, meaning from morning till midnight, decides what you are.

Do you understand what I'm saying? You must know this real fact. If you understand this fact, you can change yourself and imagine yourself in the future. You can imagine very clearly what you want to be in the future.

This is a real technique of spiritual technique and a magical technique of spiritual technique. You can be what you want to be, so the tech-nique is to just imagine or draw a picture in your mind what you really need, hope, or desire to be in the future.

When you confront difficulties, First say, "I can"

People are apt to think of a bad design, a bad future, or an evil future in their mind. I, myself, in my younger days often thought like that. Every time a bad thing came, I felt some kind of a bad future was coming to me, and I hesitated to take a positive action, or sometimes thought over my inferiority complex. "I can't do this. I cannot do this hard work. I cannot overcome this difficult problem." I usually felt like that in my younger days.

But when I found this simple Truth that, "If people really believe and think, as they use that phrase, 'I can,' they can change their future," I, myself, changed myself by these words. When you confront difficulties, please say to yourself, "I can, I can, I can." Never say, "I cannot, I cannot." It leads to nowhere, and you cannot succeed in anything. In any case, when you confront difficulties, please say, "I can."

Firstly, "I can." Next, please think about that. Firstly, "I can" or "We can." If you are asked, "Can you speak English?" never say, "I cannot speak English." It's English [*audience laughs*]. If you can say, "I cannot speak English," it's a lie because you spoke English already. So, firstly, you must say, "I can" or "We can."

4

Make Up Your Mind and Design a Beautiful Future

Be brave,
And do not fear making mistakes

Next, [*to the Japanese audience*] make effort to study English and try to convey the Truth, or dendo. At that time, you will feel a lot of emotions. You might feel some kind of criticism from foreign people. Native English speakers are honest, so they will point out your mistakes, but be brave and don't hesitate. It's not easy for foreign people to speak a foreign language. It's very difficult.

American President Barack Obama is a good speaker, and he is good at making good speeches like Lincoln or Kennedy, it is said so, but even when he makes a speech, he already has a manuscript made. Almost all of the manuscript is written by himself, but some people add some words to the manuscript. Even Mr. Obama needs a manuscript when he makes a short speech for 10 or 20 minutes, but Ryuho Okawa needs no manuscript. I can speak without a manuscript or some kind of preparation. I can speak for an hour because I was born from my mouth first. I have a microchip in my lips [*audience laughs*], so I can speak without a manuscript.

So, be brave. Don't be afraid to make a mistake. Even the American president needs some kind of manuscript, so it's usual for you to feel very difficult to speak English. Don't feel inferiority complex. You are Japanese and you can speak Japanese, so if you can speak English fluently without any preparation, you all are geniuses. You are making efforts to be a genius, so be brave.

If you can change your mind and make up your mind to speak in English, please say to yourself, "Yes, I can, I can, I can, I can, I can," or "We can, we can, we can, we can" every time you have a chance to speak English. These magical words will change you. In the near future, "Yes, you can," I promise.

Your life is decided by the direction Your mind points to

It's the key to life's golden secrets. It's true. I, myself, checked that this is true in these 20 or 30 years, so believe in me. It's true. Life is what you think you are, and life is the direction of your mind. It is your life. It decides your life.

In other words, your burning desire is yourself, so please make up your mind. You must design your future figure, I mean, what you are to be in the near future, your splendid and beautiful future, and it will come to you.

Get this Truth,
"What I can imagine is what I am"

Firstly, please forget that you are made of material things, and please think that you are what you are thinking about. You are the "imaginable" power, or imagining power. You can imagine, and that is what you are.

If you can get this Truth, "What I can imagine is what I am," you will go ahead to become a great man or woman. Angels in heaven know about this Truth, of course. They are good prayers, and their praying for the happiness of other people means that the power of the mind is a real thing, a real being.

> So, don't be materialistic
> And don't be a realist.
> Be an "imaginable" person,
> And please always look inside of you
> And think that

You are what you are thinking about.
It's the key to life's golden secrets.
That's the conclusion of today.

Afterword

"Thoughts will realize." Even if you hear this, I'm sure many of you will think that there are already so many books that talk about this.

However, I want you to read this book very carefully. This book reveals to you about "awareness as a child of God," "the importance of self-help," and "the secret to becoming a creative person."

It is not so easy to master the teaching that has both "faith in God" and "the laws of cause and effect."

In Japan, I am guiding a political party called "The Happiness Realization Party," but many of the voters lack "faith in God" and hate "self-help." Most of them think the function of democracy is to scatter tax money to the people.

Even this single book is spiritual enough that people living materialistically cannot appreciate its truth. I hope a spiritual revolution will occur through this book.

Ryuho Okawa
Master & CEO of Happy Science Group
Aug. 22, 2019

ABOUT THE AUTHOR

Founder and CEO of Happy Science Group.

Ryuho Okawa was born on July 7th 1956, in Tokushima, Japan. After graduating from the University of Tokyo with a law degree, he joined a Tokyo-based trading house. While working at its New York headquarters, he studied international finance at the Graduate Center of the City University of New York. In 1981, he attained Great Enlightenment and became aware that he is El Cantare with a mission to bring salvation to all humankind.

In 1986, he established Happy Science. It now has members in over 165 countries across the world, with more than 700 branches and temples as well as 10,000 missionary houses around the world.

He has given over 3,400 lectures (of which more than 150 are in English) and published over 3,000 books (of which more than 600 are Spiritual Interview Series), and many are translated into 40 languages. Along with *The Laws of the Sun* and *The Laws Of Messiah*, many of the books have become best sellers or million sellers. To date, Happy Science has produced 25 movies. The original story and original concept were given by the Executive Producer Ryuho Okawa. He has also composed music and written lyrics of over 450 pieces.

Moreover, he is the Founder of Happy Science University and Happy Science Academy (Junior and Senior High School), Founder and President of the Happiness Realization Party, Founder and Honorary Headmaster of Happy Science Institute of Government and Management, Founder of IRH Press Co., Ltd., and the Chairperson of NEW STAR PRODUCTION Co., Ltd. and ARI Production Co., Ltd.

WHAT IS EL CANTARE?

El Cantare means "the Light of the Earth," and is the Supreme God of the Earth who has been guiding humankind since the beginning of Genesis. He is whom Jesus called Father and Muhammad called Allah, and is *Ame-no-Mioya-Gami*, Japanese Father God. Different parts of El Cantare's core consciousness have descended to Earth in the past, once as Alpha and another as Elohim. His branch spirits, such as Shakyamuni Buddha and Hermes, have descended to Earth many times and helped to flourish many civilizations. To unite various religions and to integrate various fields of study in order to build a new civilization on Earth, a part of the core consciousness has descended to Earth as Master Ryuho Okawa.

Alpha is a part of the core consciousness of El Cantare who descended to Earth around 330 million years ago. Alpha preached Earth's Truths to harmonize and unify Earth-born humans and space people who came from other planets.

Elohim is a part of the core consciousness of El Cantare who descended to Earth around 150 million years ago. He gave wisdom, mainly on the differences of light and darkness, good and evil.

Ame-no-Mioya-Gami (Japanese Father God) is the Creator God and the Father God who appears in the ancient literature, *Hotsuma Tsutae*. It is believed that He descended on the foothills of Mt. Fuji about 30,000 years ago and built the Fuji dynasty, which is the root of the Japanese civilization. With justice as the central pillar, Ame-no-Mioya-Gami's teachings spread to ancient civilizations of other countries in the world.

Shakyamuni Buddha was born as a prince into the Shakya Clan in India around 2,600 years ago. When he was 29 years old, he renounced the world and sought enlightenment. He later attained Great Enlightenment and founded Buddhism.

Hermes is one of the 12 Olympian gods in Greek mythology, but the spiritual Truth is that he taught the teachings of love and progress around 4,300 years ago that became the origin of the current Western civilization. He is a hero that truly existed.

Ophealis was born in Greece around 6,500 years ago and was the leader who took an expedition to as far as Egypt. He is the God of miracles, prosperity, and arts, and is known as Osiris in the Egyptian mythology.

Rient Arl Croud was born as a king of the ancient Incan Empire around 7,000 years ago and taught about the mysteries of the mind. In the heavenly world, he is responsible for the interactions that take place between various planets.

Thoth was an almighty leader who built the golden age of the Atlantic civilization around 12,000 years ago. In the Egyptian mythology, he is known as god Thoth.

Ra Mu was a leader who built the golden age of the civilization of Mu around 17,000 years ago. As a religious leader and a politician, he ruled by uniting religion and politics.

ABOUT HAPPY SCIENCE

Happy Science is a global movement that empowers individuals to find purpose and spiritual happiness and to share that happiness with their families, societies, and the world. With more than 12 million members around the world, Happy Science aims to increase awareness of spiritual truths and expand our capacity for love, compassion, and joy so that together we can create the kind of world we all wish to live in.

Activities at Happy Science are based on the Principle of Happiness (Love, Wisdom, Self-Reflection, and Progress). This principle embraces worldwide philosophies and beliefs, transcending boundaries of culture and religions.

> **Love** teaches us to give ourselves freely without expecting anything in return; it encompasses giving, nurturing, and forgiving.
>
> **Wisdom** leads us to the insights of spiritual truths, and opens us to the true meaning of life and the will of God (the universe, the highest power, Buddha).
>
> **Self-Reflection** brings a mindful, nonjudgmental lens to our thoughts and actions to help us find our truest selves—the essence of our souls—and deepen our connection to the highest power. It helps us attain a clean and peaceful mind and leads us to the right life path.

Progress emphasizes the positive, dynamic aspects of our spiritual growth—actions we can take to manifest and spread happiness around the world. It's a path that not only expands our soul growth, but also furthers the collective potential of the world we live in.

PROGRAMS AND EVENTS

The doors of Happy Science are open to all. We offer a variety of programs and events, including self-exploration and self-growth programs, spiritual seminars, meditation and contemplation sessions, study groups, and book events.

Our programs are designed to:
* Deepen your understanding of your purpose and meaning in life
* Improve your relationships and increase your capacity to love unconditionally
* Attain peace of mind, decrease anxiety and stress, and feel positive
* Gain deeper insights and a broader perspective on the world
* Learn how to overcome life's challenges
   ... and much more.

For more information, visit happy-science.org.

OUR ACTIVITIES

Happy Science does other various activities to provide support for those in need.

- **You Are An Angel! General Incorporated Association**

    Happy Science has a volunteer network in Japan that encourages and supports children with disabilities as well as their parents and guardians.

- **Never Mind School for Truancy**

    At 'Never Mind,' we support students who find it very challenging to attend schools in Japan. We also nurture their self-help spirit and power to rebound against obstacles in life based on Master Okawa's teachings and faith.

- **"Prevention Against Suicide" Campaign since 2003**

    A nationwide campaign to reduce suicides; over 20,000 people commit suicide every year in Japan. "The Suicide Prevention Website-Words of Truth for You-" presents spiritual prescriptions for worries such as depression, lost love, extramarital affairs, bullying and work-related problems, thereby saving many lives.

- **Support for Anti-bullying Campaigns**

    Happy Science provides support for a group of parents and guardians, Network to Protect Children from Bullying, a general incorporated foundation launched in Japan to end bullying, including those that can even be called a criminal offense. So far, the network received more than 5,000 cases and resolved 90% of them.

- **The Golden Age Scholarship**
  This scholarship is granted to students who can contribute greatly and bring a hopeful future to the world.

- **Success No.1**
  Buddha's Truth Afterschool Academy
  Happy Science has over 180 classrooms throughout Japan and in several cities around the world that focus on afterschool education for children. The education focuses on faith and morals in addition to supporting children's school studies.

- **Angel Plan V**
  For children under the age of kindergarten, Happy Science holds classes for nurturing healthy, positive, and creative boys and girls.

- **Future Stars Training Department**
  The Future Stars Training Department was founded within the Happy Science Media Division with the goal of nurturing talented individuals to become successful in the performing arts and entertainment industry.

- **NEW STAR PRODUCTION Co., Ltd.**
  ARI Production Co., Ltd.
  We have companies to nurture actors and actresses, artists, and vocalists. They are also involved in film production.

CONTACT INFORMATION

Happy Science is a worldwide organization with branches and temples around the globe. For a comprehensive list, visit the worldwide directory at *happy-science.org*. The following are some of the many Happy Science locations:

UNITED STATES AND CANADA

New York
79 Franklin St., New York, NY 10013, USA
Phone: 1-212-343-7972
Fax: 1-212-343-7973
Email: ny@happy-science.org
Website: happyscience-usa.org

New Jersey
66 Hudson St., #2R, Hoboken, NJ 07030, USA
Phone: 1-201-313-0127
Email: nj@happy-science.org
Website: happyscience-usa.org

Chicago
2300 Barrington Rd., Suite #400,
Hoffman Estates, IL 60169, USA
Phone: 1-630-937-3077
Email: chicago@happy-science.org
Website: happyscience-usa.org

Florida
5208 8th St., Zephyrhills, FL 33542, USA
Phone: 1-813-715-0000
Fax: 1-813-715-0010
Email: florida@happy-science.org
Website: happyscience-usa.org

Atlanta
1874 Piedmont Ave., NE Suite 360-C
Atlanta, GA 30324, USA
Phone: 1-404-892-7770
Email: atlanta@happy-science.org
Website: happyscience-usa.org

San Francisco
525 Clinton St. Redwood City, CA 94062, USA
Phone & Fax: 1-650-363-2777
Email: sf@happy-science.org
Website: happyscience-usa.org

Los Angeles
1590 E. Del Mar Blvd., Pasadena, CA 91106, USA
Phone: 1-626-395-7775
Fax: 1-626-395-7776
Email: la@happy-science.org
Website: happyscience-usa.org

Orange County
16541 Gothard St. Suite 104
Huntington Beach, CA 92647
Phone: 1-714-659-1501
Email: oc@happy-science.org
Website: happyscience-usa.org

San Diego
7841 Balboa Ave. Suite #202
San Diego, CA 92111, USA
Phone: 1-626-395-7775
Fax: 1-626-395-7776
E-mail: sandiego@happy-science.org
Website: happyscience-usa.org

Hawaii
Phone: 1-808-591-9772
Fax: 1-808-591-9776
Email: hi@happy-science.org
Website: happyscience-usa.org

Kauai
3343 Kanakolu Street, Suite 5
Lihue, HI 96766, USA
Phone: 1-808-822-7007
Fax: 1-808-822-6007
Email: kauai-hi@happy-science.org
Website: happyscience-usa.org

Toronto
845 The Queensway Etobicoke,
ON M8Z 1N6, Canada
Phone: 1-416-901-3747
Email: toronto@happy-science.org
Website: happy-science.ca

Vancouver
#201-2607 East 49th Avenue,
Vancouver, BC, V5S 1J9, Canada
Phone: 1-604-437-7735
Fax: 1-604-437-7764
Email: vancouver@happy-science.org
Website: happy-science.ca

INTERNATIONAL

Tokyo
1-6-7 Togoshi, Shinagawa,
Tokyo, 142-0041, Japan
Phone: 81-3-6384-5770
Fax: 81-3-6384-5776
Email: tokyo@happy-science.org
Website: happy-science.org

Seoul
74, Sadang-ro 27-gil, Dongjak-gu,
Seoul, Korea
Phone: 82-2-3478-8777
Fax: 82-2-3478-9777
Email: korea@happy-science.org
Website: happyscience-korea.org

London
3 Margaret St.London,
W1W 8RE United Kingdom
Phone: 44-20-7323-9255
Fax: 44-20-7323-9344
Email: eu@happy-science.org
Website: www.happyscience-uk.org

Taipei
No. 89, Lane 155, Dunhua N. Road,
Songshan District, Taipei City 105, Taiwan
Phone: 886-2-2719-9377
Fax: 886-2-2719-5570
Email: taiwan@happy-science.org
Website: happyscience-tw.org

Sydney
516 Pacific Highway, Lane Cove North,
2066 NSW, Australia
Phone: 61-2-9411-2877
Fax: 61-2-9411-2822
Email: sydney@happy-science.org

Kuala Lumpur
No 22A, Block 2, Jalil Link Jalan Jalil
Jaya 2, Bukit Jalil 57000,
Kuala Lumpur, Malaysia
Phone: 60-3-8998-7877
Fax: 60-3-8998-7977
Email: malaysia@happy-science.org
Website: happyscience.org.my

Sao Paulo
Rua. Domingos de Morais 1154,
Vila Mariana, Sao Paulo SP
CEP 04010-100, Brazil
Phone: 55-11-5088-3800
Email: sp@happy-science.org
Website: happyscience.com.br

Kathmandu
Kathmandu Metropolitan City,
Ward No. 15, Ring Road, Kimdol,
Sitapaila Kathmandu, Nepal
Phone: 977-1-427-2931
Email: nepal@happy-science.org

Jundiai
Rua Congo, 447, Jd. Bonfiglioli
Jundiai-CEP, 13207-340, Brazil
Phone: 55-11-4587-5952
Email: jundiai@happy-science.org

Kampala
Plot 877 Rubaga Road, Kampala
P.O. Box 34130 Kampala, UGANDA
Phone: 256-79-4682-121
Email: uganda@happy-science.org

ABOUT HS PRESS

HS Press is an imprint of IRH Press Co., Ltd. IRH Press Co., Ltd., based in Tokyo, was founded in 1987 as a publishing division of Happy Science. IRH Press publishes religious and spiritual books, journals, magazines and also operates broadcast and film production enterprises. For more information, visit *okawabooks.com*.

Follow us on:

- Facebook: Okawa Books
- Youtube: Okawa Books
- Pinterest: Okawa Books
- Instagram: OkawaBooks
- Twitter: Okawa Books
- Goodreads: Ryuho Okawa

NEWSLETTER

To receive book related news, promotions and events, please subscribe to our newsletter below.

🔗 eepurl.com/bsMeJj

AUDIO / VISUAL MEDIA

YOUTUBE — **PODCAST**

Introduction of Ryuho Okawa's titles; topics ranging from self-help, current affairs, spirituality, religion, and the universe.

BOOKS BY RYUHO OKAWA

RYUHO OKAWA'S LAWS SERIES

The Laws Series is an annual volume of books that are mainly comprised of Ryuho Okawa's lectures that function as universal guidance to all people. They are of various topics that were given in accordance with the changes that each year brings. *The Laws of the Sun*, the first publication of the laws series, ranked in the annual best-selling list in Japan in 1994. Since, the laws series' titles have ranked in the annual best-selling list every year for more than two decades, setting socio-cultural trends in Japan and around the world.

The 28th Laws Series
The Laws Of Messiah
From Love to Love

Paperback • 248 pages • $16.95
ISBN: 978-1-942125-90-7 (Jan. 31, 2022)

"What is Messiah?" This book carries an important message of love and guidance to people living now from the Modern-Day Messiah or the Modern-Day Savior. It also reveals the secret of Shambhala, the spiritual center of Earth, as well as the truth that this spiritual center is currently in danger of perishing and what we can do to protect this sacred place.

Love your Lord God. Know that those who don't know love don't know God. Discover the true love of God and the ideal practice of faith. This book teaches the most important element we must not lose sight of as we go through our soul training on Earth.

THE LAWS OF THE SUN
ONE SOURCE, ONE PLANET, ONE PEOPLE

Paperback • 288 pages • $15.95
ISBN: 978-1-942125-43-3

Imagine if you could ask God why he created this world and what spiritual laws he used to shape us—and everything around us. In The Laws of the Sun, Ryuho Okawa outlines these laws of the universe and provides a road map for living one's life with greater purpose and meaning. This powerful book shows the way to realize true happiness—a happiness that continues from this world through the other.

THE LAWS OF SUCCESS
A SPIRITUAL GUIDE TO TURNING YOUR HOPES INTO REALITY

Paperback • 208 pages • $15.95
ISBN: 978-1-942125-15-0

The Laws of Success offers 8 spiritual principles that, when put to practice in our day-to-day life, will help us attain lasting success and let us experience the fulfillment of living our purpose and the joy of sharing our happiness with many others. The timeless wisdom and practical steps that Ryuho Okawa offers will guide us through any difficulties and problems we may face in life, and serve as guiding principles for living a positive, constructive, and meaningful life.

For a complete list of books, visit okawabooks.com

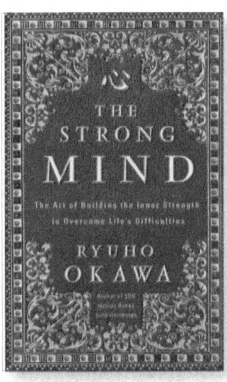

THE STRONG MIND
THE ART OF BUILDING THE INNER STRENGTH TO OVERCOME LIFE'S DIFFICULTIES

Paperback • 192 pages • $15.95
ISBN: 978-1-942125-36-5

The strong mind is what we need to rise time and again, and to move forward no matter what difficulties we face in life. This book will inspire and empower you to take courage, develop a mature and cultivated heart, and achieve resilience and hardiness so that you can break through the barriers of your limits and keep winning in the battle of your life.

WORRY-FREE LIVING
LET GO OF STRESS AND LIVE IN PEACE AND HAPPINESS

Hardcover • 192 pages • $16.95
ISBN: 978-1-942125-51-8

The wisdom Ryuho Okawa shares in this book about facing problems in human relationships, financial hardships, and other life's stresses will help you change how you look at and approach life's worries and problems for the better. Let this book be your guide to finding precious meaning in all your life's problems, gaining inner growth no matter what you face, and practicing inner happiness and soul-growth all throughout your life.

For a complete list of books, visit okawabooks.com

INVINCIBLE THINKING
AN ESSENTIAL GUIDE FOR A LIFETIME OF GROWTH, SUCCESS, AND TRIUMPH

Hardcover • 208 pages • $16.95
ISBN: 978-1-942125-25-9

In this book, Ryuho Okawa lays out the principles of invincible thinking that will allow us to achieve long-lasting triumph. This powerful and unique philosophy is not only about becoming successful or achieving our goal in life, but also about building the foundation of life that becomes the basis of our life-long, lasting success and happiness.

THINK BIG!

BE POSITIVE AND BE BRAVE TO ACHIEVE YOUR DREAMS

Hardcover • 160 pages • $12.95
ISBN: 978-1-942125-04-4

Think Big! offers the support and encouragement to shift to new ways of thinking and mastering self-discipline. The self-proven approach fosters stability and strength in the challenges each of us faces. In addition to his relatable stories and a motivational voice to keep us going, each chapter builds on the next for concrete methodologies that, when added up, are a track to support your dreams, yourself, and your life.

For a complete list of books, visit okawabooks.com

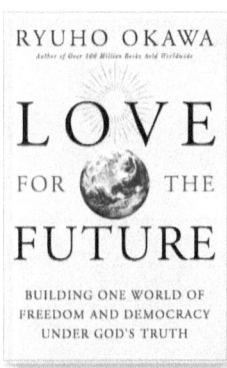

LOVE FOR THE FUTURE
BUILDING ONE WORLD OF FREEDOM AND DEMOCRACY UNDER GOD'S TRUTH

Paperback • 312 pages • $15.95
ISBN: 978-1-942125-60-0

This is a compilation of select international lectures given by Ryuho Okawa during his (ongoing) global missionary tours. While conflicting values of justice exists, this book espouses that freedom and democracy are vital principles for global unification that will resolutely foster peace and shared prosperity, if adopted universally.

SPIRITUAL MESSAGES FROM JAMES ALLEN
THE TRUE MEANING OF HAPPINESS AND SUCCESS

Paperback • 104 pages • $9.95
ISBN: 978-1-94386-936-7

James Allen wrote As a Man Thinketh, often considered the greatest self-help book in the world, in 1903. What advice would he give to the modern people if he lived in 2017, more than a century after his days? Spiritual Messages from James Allen: The True Meaning of Happiness and Success shows the answer.

For a complete list of books, visit okawabooks.com

MUSIC BY RYUHO OKAWA

El Cantare Ryuho Okawa Original Songs

A song celebrating Lord God

A song celebrating Lord God,
the God of the Earth,
who is beyond a prophet.

The Water Revolution
English and Chinese version

For the truth and happiness of the 1.4 billion people in China who have no freedom. Love, justice, and sacred rage of God are on this melody that will give you courage to fight to bring peace.

Search on YouTube

> the water revolution for a short ad!

Listen now today!
Download from
 Spotify **iTunes** **Amazon**

DVD, CD available at amazon.com, and Happy Science locations worldwide

With Savior *English version*

This is the message of hope to the modern people who are living in the midst of the Coronavirus pandemic, natural disasters, economic depression, and other various crises.

Search on YouTube

| with savior | for a short ad!

The Thunder
a composition for repelling the Coronavirus

We have been granted this music from our Lord. It will repel away the novel Coronavirus originated in China. Experience this magnificent powerful music.

Search on YouTube

| the thunder composition |

for a short ad!

The Exorcism
prayer music for repelling Lost Spirits

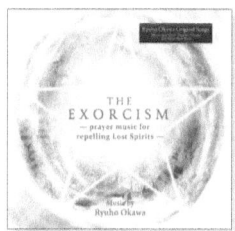

Feel the divine vibrations of this Japanese and Western exorcising symphony to banish all evil possessions you suffer from and to purify your space!

Search on YouTube

| the exorcism repelling |

for a short ad!

Listen now today!
Download from
Spotify iTunes Amazon

DVD, CD available at amazon.com, and Happy Science locations worldwide

www.ingramcontent.com/pod-product-compliance
Lightning Source LLC
Chambersburg PA
CBHW030157100526
44592CB00009B/328